As brilliant as a peacock, the **harlequin tuskfish** (*Choerodon fasciatus*) is really quite shy. Typically, it has orange, blue-edged bands, three on the head and five on the body. Even its teeth are colorful, with bright blue points.

3

The **saddled butterflyfish** (*Chaetodon ephippium*), lower left and bottom right, resembles an angelfish in shape. It is gray and blue, with a yellow underside and has a large, white-bordered black patch on its back. The **copperband butterflyfish** (*Chelmon rostratus*), top

right and middle left, has a large black spot on its back. Resembling an eye, it confuses predators. It picks up food with its long snout. The **pig-faced butterflyfish** (*Chaetodon falcula*), middle, has a similar eye-like marking on its yellow back.

The orange, white-striped **clownfish** *(Amphiprion percula)*, is named for its waddling movement. The clownfish is one of the few species of fish which can avoid the dangerous stings of the sea anemone, and it cleans the anemone by eating accumulated plankton. The female clownfish lives with a group of males. When she dies, a male changes sex, becoming the new female.

The **giant cuttlefish** (*Sepia apama*) is related to the octopus. It has the ability to change color, and the males, when courting females, put on a dazzling show of vivid, pulsating stripes.

The **olive sea snake** (*Aipysurus laevis*) breathes air, like its cousin the cobra. However, the sea snake can stay underwater for twenty or more hours.

The **blue tang** *(Paracanthuras hepatus)* has a striking royal blue body with black markings and a brilliant yellow tail. An herbivore, it helps keep the algae population from suffocating the coral reef.

Regal angelfish (*Pygoplites diacanthus*) are among the showiest Barrier Reef fish, with alternating blue, yellow and black stripes. They grow to a foot in length.

This juvenile **rock-mover wrasse** (*Novaculichthys taeniorus*)
digs and burrows vigorously into sediment to escape predators.

Nudibranchs are shell-less snails or **sea slugs.** To deter predators, they have evolved with glorious colors which serve to camouflage them or convey messages of distaste or danger. *Tambja affinis,* top left, has yellow and dark blue stripes, with patches of blue-green. *Casella atromarginata,* bottom left, is tan and white, with a white-bordered black "ruffle." *Nembrotha nudibranch,* at bottom right, is black with green spots. *Chromodoris coi,* middle right, is white and tan, bisected by a wavy black stripe. The red-orange **Spanish dancer** (*Hexabranchus sanguineus*), top right, is the largest of all the nudibranchs, growing from 2½ inches to 2½ feet.

The beautiful orange and blue **mandarin fish** (*Synchiropus splen-didus*), covered in kaleidoscopic patterns, is a shy fish that nonethe-less exhibits prolonged and elaborate courtship behavior. Here, they swim in front of **whip gorgonian coral** (*Junceella juncea*).

The carnivorous **clown triggerfish** (*Balistoides conspicillum*) is black with large white spots. Its vivid yellow mouth warns predators to keep their distance. Here, they swim among **sea fans,** also called **gorgonians.**

15

The handsome **Moorish idol** *(Zanclus cornutus)*, banded in black, white, and yellow, has a sickle-shaped dorsal fin which grows shorter with age.

The beautiful green **moon wrasse** (*Thalassoma lunare*) has
bright pink pectoral fins with blue edges. This male swims
in front of a **feather starfish,** a **crinoid.**

Dark green, brown or gray, with vivid diagonal stripes, the **orange-lined triggerfish** (*Balistapus undulatus*) is solitary, and most active during the day. To keep from being pulled away or swallowed whole, it locks or unlocks its dorsal spines.

The tiny red and blue **loki whip-goby** *(Bryaninops loki)*, less than two inches long, lives on sponges and corals. Here, one swims past a **sea whip coral** *(Muricea muricata)*, which is a collection of hundreds of individual animals, or polyps.

Two feet long, the **bluespine unicornfish** (*Naso unicornus*) has a bony protrusion on his head as well as sharp spines near the tail. Here, he swims past soft coral.

The **scribbled angelfish** (*Chaetodontoplus duboulayi*),
nearly a foot long, has beautiful blue coloring with dark wavy
lines. The head and tail have yellow and white bands.

21

Usually a foot and a half long, the **saber squirrelfish** (*Sargocentron spiniferum*) has red scales with white margins. The largest of the squirrelfish, it attacks predators with a venomous spine in its cheek.

The **tiger shark** (*Galeocerdo cuvier*) can grow up to more than fourteen feet long and weigh up to 1,400 pounds. It is second only to the great white shark in its number of attacks on humans. The stripes on its back fade as the shark ages. Hunting in both deep and shallow waters, it eats nearly anything, including license plates, rubber tires and tennis balls.

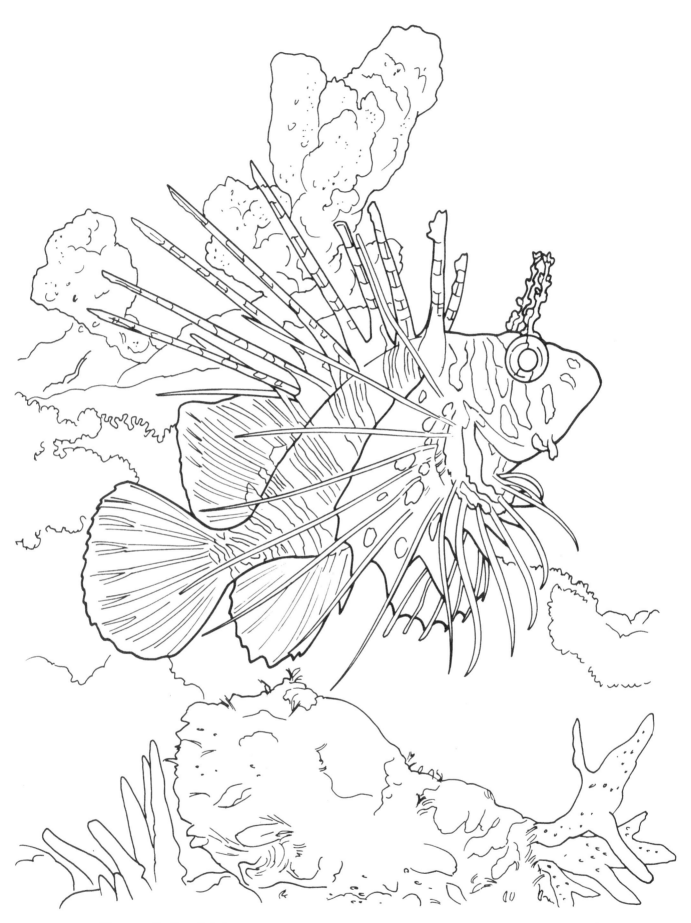

The **spotfin lionfish** (*Pterois antennata*), growing to about eight inches, is known by its alternating broad and narrow dark red bands. It swallows its prey whole. Its fin spines can cause painful wounds to humans. Here, the lionfish swims by marine sponges.

Measuring twenty inches in diameter at most, the reddish **crown-of-thorns starfish** (*Acanthaster planci*) is nonetheless an efficient and deadly predator. Its slim, sharp, toxin-filled spines glide easily into prey, causing death or injury. These starfish can also destroy coral reef very quickly.

25

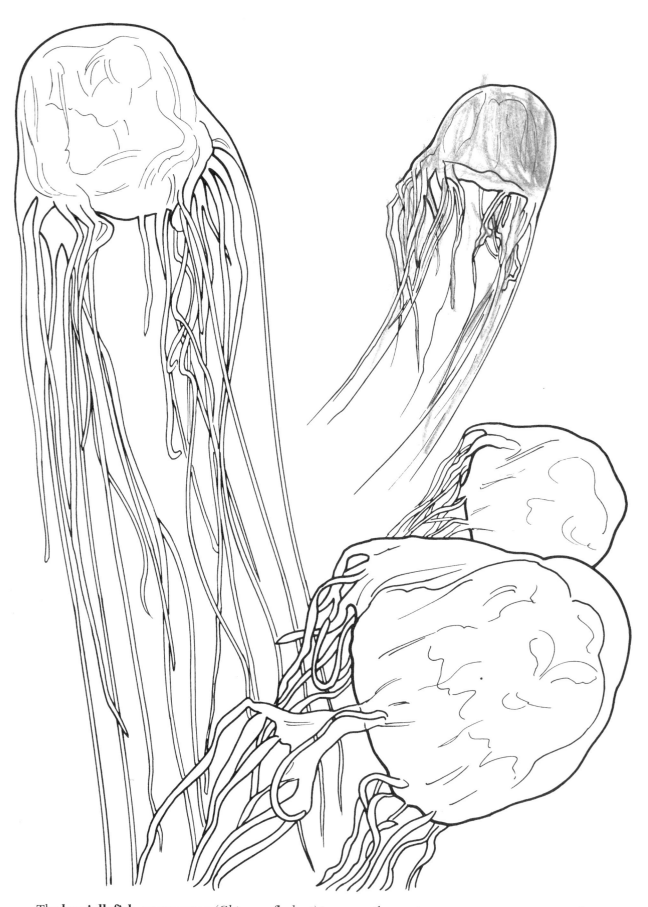

The **box jellyfish,** or **sea wasp** *(Chironex fleckeri)* is among the most venomous creatures on earth. It feeds on shrimps, instantly immobilizing its prey with the strong poison on its tentacles. While the box jellyfish does not attack humans, a swimmer may inadvertently bump into one. The most dangerous time to encounter one is between November and April—the wet season. It is estimated that more than 67 people have been killed by these creatures during the last century.

The **blue-ringed octopus** (*Octopus maculosus*) is normally brown, and about the size of a golf ball. However, when agitated, it becomes vivid yellow with blue rings and spreads to about seven inches. The venom in its saliva can easily kill a human. Some scientists claim that octopuses are the most intelligent of the invertebrates.

About six feet long and nearly two hundred pounds, the **potato cod** (*Epinephelus tukula*), blue-gray with dark spots, has such a large mouth and powerful jaws that it swallows whole shrimp, octopus, and squid.

Growing up to eight feet in length, the **yellow-edge moray eel** (*Lycodontis flavimarginatus*) is ochre, with dark brown mottling, and is named for the border on its fins. It is often drawn to reefs after a fish has been speared, perhaps because of its unusual sensitivity to the stress emanating from an injured fish.

Noted for its bright red dorsal fin, pale orange body, and lavender head, the male **redfin anthias** *(Pseudanthias dispar)*, top, swims with females several feet above the ocean floor. It grows to less than four inches in length. The **redbar anthias** *(Pseudanthias rubrizonatus)*, middle, is about the same size, but has a striking red band on its cream body. At bottom, the male **purple anthias** *(Pseudanthias tuka)* has yellow markings on its underside. It can reach nearly five inches.